Families

Cousins

Rebecca Rissman

Raintree

www.raintreepublishers.co.uk
Visit our website to find out
more information about
Raintree books.

To order:
☎ Phone 0845 6044371
🖶 Fax +44 (0) 1865 312263
🖥 Email myorders@raintreepublishers.co.uk

Customers from outside the UK please telephone +44 1865 312262

Raintree is an imprint of Capstone Global Library Limited, a company incorporated in England and Wales having its registered office at 7 Pilgrim Street, London, EC4V 6LB – Registered company number: 6695582

Edited by Rebecca Rissman, Dan Nunn, and Catherine Veitch
Designed by Ryan Frieson
Picture research by Tracy Cummins
Production by Victoria Fitzgerald
Originated by Capstone Global Library
Printed and bound in China by Leo Paper Products Ltd

ISBN 978 1 406 22146 6
14 13 12 11 10
10 9 8 7 6 5 4 3 2 1

British Library Cataloguing in Publication Data
Rissman, Rebecca.
Cousins. -- (Families)
306.8'7-dc22

Acknowledgements
We would like to thank the following for permission to reproduce photographs:
Corbis pp. **7** (©LWA-Sharie Kennedy), **14** (©Heide Benser); Getty Images pp. **6** and **8** (both Jupiterimages), **9** (Andersen Ross), **10** (Jack Hollingsworth), **11** (Camille Tokerud) **13** (Antenna), **17** (RPM Pictures), **18** (Tony Metaxas), **23 b** (Camille Tokerud), **23 d** (Jack Hollingsworth); istockphoto pp. **5** (©Duane Ellison), **15** (©kzenon), **19** (©Linda Kloosterhof), **20** (©Carmen Martínez Banús), **22** (©Diane Labombarbe), **23 a** (©Carmen Martínez Banús); Photolibrary pp. **12** and **23 c** (both Kevin Dodge); Shutterstock pp. **4** (©Michael Jung), **16** (©Morgan Lane Photography), **21** (©Kim Ruoff).

Front cover photograph of three children embracing with permission of Getty Images (Sami Sarkis). Back cover photograph of children in a tent reproduced with permission of Shutterstock (© Morgan Lane Photography).

We would like to thank Anne Pezalla, Diana Bentley, and Dee Reid for their invaluable help in the preparation of this book.

Every effort has been made to contact copyright holders of material reproduced in this book. Any omissions will be rectified in subsequent printings if notice is given to the publisher.

Contents

What is a family?

A family is a group of people who care for each other.

People in families are called
family members.

All families are different.

All families are special.

What are families like?

Some families are large.

Some families are small.

Who are aunts and uncles?

Some families have aunts and uncles.

Aunts and uncles are your parents' sisters and brothers.

Who are cousins?

If your aunts and uncles have children, they are your cousins.

Cousins can be boys or girls.

Different cousins

Some families have many cousins.

Some families have no cousins.

Some cousins live near by.
Some cousins live far away.

Some cousins look alike.

Some cousins look different.

Some cousins live with their parents.

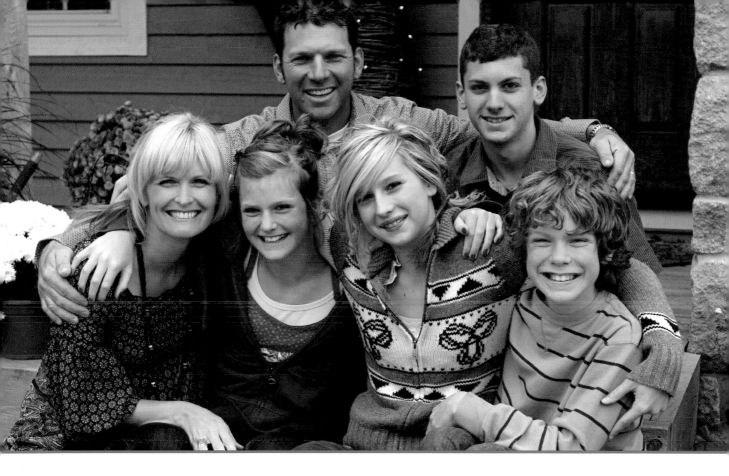

Some cousins live with different family members.

Some cousins are adopted.

They have joined a new family.

Do you have cousins?

Family tree

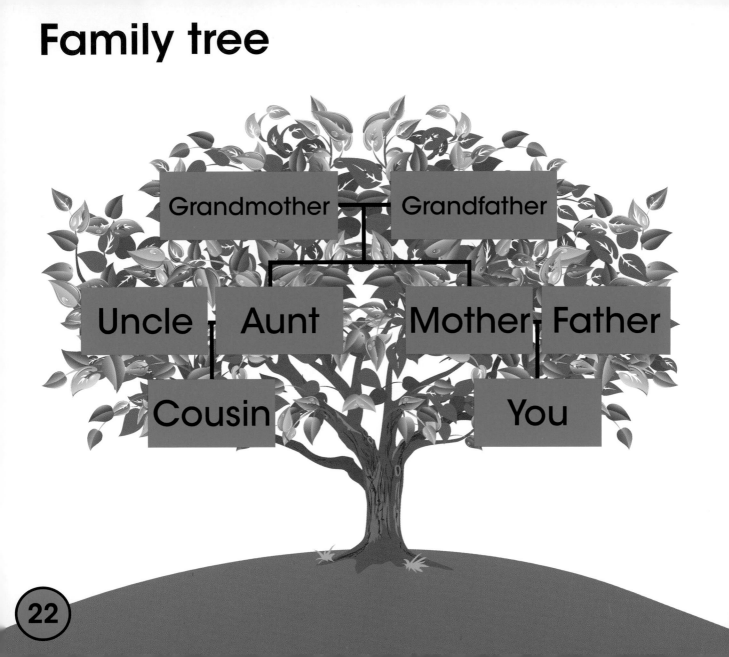

Picture glossary

adopted invited to join a new family. Many children are adopted by new families.

aunt a parent's sister

cousin child of an aunt or uncle

uncle a parent's brother

Index

Note to parents and teachers

Before reading

Open the book to page 22 and show children the family tree graphic. Explain to children that the lines connecting the different boxes represent relationships. Then use this graphic to explain how they are related to their parents, their grandparents, their aunts and uncles, and their cousins.

After reading

Ask children to raise their hands if they have aunts or uncles. Then ask children to raise their hands if they have any cousins. Engage the class in a contest to see who has the most cousins. Ask children to raise their hand if they have one cousin, two cousins, three cousins, etc, until only one child has his or her hand raised. Ask this child how many cousins he or she has!